Puffin Books

The Puffin Book of Australian Mammals

In this book you will find out about Australian mammals from A to Z. There are bats, rats, kangaroos, whales and possums, as well as lesser-known and vanishing mammals like quokkas, dunnarts and dugongs, and those thought to be extinct, such as the Tasmanian tiger. They are identified with a drawing or colour photograph, and the author describes different families and species – their characteristics, where they live, what they eat and how you can study them safely.

Arranged alphabetically and with an index, this book is a must for all who want to share with Helen Hunt in a wider understanding of Australia's natural world.

Other Books in This Series

The Puffin Book of Australian Mammals

Helen Hunt

Puffin Books

Puffin Books
Penguin Books Australia Ltd
487 Maroondah Highway, PO Box 257
Ringwood, Victoria, 3134, Australia
Penguin Books Ltd
Harmondsworth, Middlesex, England
Viking Penguin, A Division of Penguin Books USA Inc.
375 Hudson Street, New York, New York 10014, USA
Penguin Books Canada Limited
10 Alcorn Avenue, Toronto, Ontario, Canada M4V 1E4
Penguin Books (N.Z.) Ltd
182-190 Wairau Road, Auckland 10, New Zealand

First published 1980 by Lothian Publishing Company Pty Ltd.
Published in Puffin 1990
Copyright © Helen Hunt, 1980

10 9 8 7 6 5 4 3 2

Typeset in 10 point Times by Leader Composition Pty Ltd
Offset from the Lothian Publishing Company edition
Made and printed in Hong Kong by Bookbuilders Ltd

National Library of Australia
Cataloguing-in-Publication data:

Hunt, Helen, 1932–
    The Puffin book of Australian mammals.

ISBN 0 14 034210 9.

I. Mammals – Australia – Juvenile literature. I. Title.
II Title: The alphamammal book. II. Title: Australian
mammals.

599.0994

Acknowledgements

My sincere thanks go to Dr Basil Marlow, Curator of Mammals at the Australian Museum, Sydney, N.S.W. for very kindly reading my MS and offering comments.

For the many detailed and accurate black and white line drawings throughout the book I sincerely thank Marianne Blowes. For the other black and white illustrations I thank the National Library of Australia, Canberra, A.C.T. and gratefully acknowledge the use of a number of paintings from the collection of John Gould and the painting of the fruit bats by Helena Forde from the collection by Gerard Krefft. I also thank the staff of the Pictorial Library for their help.

My thanks go to Charlotte Short for the two drawings of whales and to Shannon Swinton for making the map.

For two of the colour pictures I thank the National Parks and Wildlife Service of N.S.W. and gratefully acknowledge the photo by Graham Robertson.

About the **S**tars* and the **M**ap

On most pages of this book you will find stars.
* A star means there is a black and white picture.
If there is a colour photo, it will say so in the text.

Here is a map of Australia, New Zealand and parts of
New Guinea. Put an X on the map where you live (ask
someone to help you if you are not quite sure!). Then
when you read in this book that a mammal lives in the
north-east of Australia or the S. or in Western Australia
(W.A.) you can look on the map and see where *its*
home is and if it is anywhere near *your* home. You
could look out for mammals that live near you, but
remember most mammals are shy and many sleep all
day.

Anteater — *spiny*

KINDS: The spiny anteater is also called the echidna but 'spiny anteater' is perhaps a better name because it tells us two things about the animal, doesn't it? The spiny anteater belongs in a family of its own in the Order Monotremata (see ORDERS OF MAMMALS) and with the platypus (see PLATYPUS) makes up the whole Order. A spiny anteater* is about 30cm long and weighs about 6kg. It has a bare tube-like snout and one toe on each hind foot has a long claw for scratching in between the spines. It is covered with coarse brown hair and has sharp spines on its sides and back. The ones on the back are about 6cm long and strong enough to move a big rock. The spines of the Tasmanian spiny anteater are almost covered by its long hair.

HOME: Spiny anteaters are found only in Australia and New Guinea. They live in most places but are rarely seen. It is thought that the female (see WORDS) lays her egg straight into her own pouch. When the young one hatches it feeds on milk and stays in the pouch until its spines grow, then it is put out into a hiding place (colour photos 1 and 2). (See MAMMAL—Monotreme.)

FOOD: A spiny anteater eats ants! It also eats termites or 'white-ants' as they are often called. It digs into a nest with its spade-like claws and laps up the ants or the termites with its long sticky tongue.

GENERAL: In the daytime a spiny anteater moves about making snuffling noises as it hunts for its food. If the weather is cold it curls up in a log or under a rock and sleeps or hibernates and can go without food for a month or more.

If anything attacks an anteater it digs rapidly into the ground or wedges itself underneath a rock.

Antechinus (say it like this—ant/e/kine/us)

KINDS: Antechinuses are mouse-sized marsupials (see MAMMAL) related to dunnarts (see DUNNART) and belong to the same family as native cats (see ORDERS OF MAMMALS and NATIVE CAT). They usually have thin short-haired tails and broad feet. Pigmy antechinuses or planigales are very tiny and have flattened heads (see JUST FOR FUN—Records). Antechinuses and dunnarts are often called marsupial mice but unlike mice they are not rodents (see RAT). They have 14 teeth (see colour photo 4), foxy little faces, make hissing noises and may have a pouch for their young. There are about 12 species of antechinuses and 4 kinds of planigales. Here are a few of them.

SPECIES	COLOUR	HABITS
Yellow-footed*	grey-reddish brown/ yellowish eye ring	forests E. and S./can walk upside-down
Brown	brown-grey	E./caves and forests
Little red	coppery red	N.W./grassland
Ingrams planigale	grey/short fur	N./woods and plains

Also see VANISHING MAMMALS

HOME: Antechinuses are shy little animals which are rarely seen but are found all over Australia. They live among fallen leaves and twigs, in cracks of dried ground, in grass tussocks and many other places. They mostly make a nest in a stump or in a hollow in the ground. The young ones are carried around hanging onto the mother's fur when they are too big for the pouch.

FOOD: Antechinuses eat insects, birds, lizards and mice.

GENERAL: The Latinized (see WORDS) name 'antechinus' tells us that the fur of these animals is bristly-looking.

Bandicoot

GENERAL: Are you as 'lousy as a bandicoot' or as 'bald as a bandicoot' or do you just 'bandicoot your potato patch'?! Read on to find out why we use these expressions.

Bandicoots, like kangaroos and possums, have a combing toe on each hind foot where the second and third toes are joined together but both toenails show. With this toe bandicoots groom themselves and also scratch at the ticks and lice which always infect them.

Most bandicoots live alone in a territory (see WORDS) but they visit other bandicoots. Male bandicoots will fight and kill other males which come into their territory.

HOME: Bandicoots are found in Australia and New Guinea. They live in thick bushland and are not often seen. They sleep all day in a nest of grass and twigs in a hollow in the ground or in a burrow. Usually female bandicoots have a litter (see WORDS) of 4 or 5 about twice a year. The young crawl into her backward-opening pouch and attach themselves to her teats (see MAMMAL—Marsupial).

KINDS: There are about 15 species of bandicoots but some are rare (see VANISHING MAMMALS). All bandicoots are rabbit-sized and have long noses but the group of short-nosed bandicoots have shorter noses and ears than the group of long-nosed bandicoots. Short-nosed bandicoots have spiny fur which falls out easily and may leave bald patches. The brown short-nosed bandicoot or quenda is now rare in many places but may still be seen around Perth W.A. The eastern long-nosed bandicoot* is common around Sydney N.S.W.

FOOD: Bandicoots dig for insects, roots and bulbs to eat. They also eat lizards and other small animals.

Bat

GENERAL: Do people sometimes say that you have 'bats in the belfry' or that you are 'batty'? They say things like that to me and they often tell me I am as 'blind as a bat'. Bats do sometimes live in church belfries and in houses but they are not really blind. In fact, fruit bats (see FRUIT BAT) see very well. Other bats do not see as well but they do not need to as they have a special sense called echo-location or radar by which they guide themselves through the darkness. This is how it works: a bat beams out ultrasonic clicks, which we cannot hear, through either its nose-leaf or its mouth. It then listens for the echoes which bounce back from objects the sounds hit. From the echoes the bat can tell many things, such as the size of the object, how far away it is and in which direction. As the bat flies closer to an object it increases the number of clicks so that it can catch it if it is an insect or avoid it if it is a rock. Bats can fly through fine mesh wire without touching it when they are using echo-location, so you need never fear that a bat will fly into anything as big as you! A bat's wings are made of a double piece of skin which covers the arms up to the wrists. The fingers are very long and stiffen the wings like the ribs of an umbrella but the thumb is free*. Some bats fly at 24 to 32km/h.

Bats are remarkable little animals because they are the only mammals which can truly fly. Some of them may look 'ugly' but all bats in Australia are harmless and are very useful as they eat huge quantities of insects.

Under a bat-banding scheme in America it was found that bats live from 8 to 20 years. Many spend most of their lives around the same cave or camp but some bats migrate or fly away to a warmer climate each winter, sometimes travelling long distances. How they find their way there and back in darkness is not known.

4

KINDS: There are about 2000 species of bats with about 50 kinds in Australia. They belong to the Order Chiroptera (see ORDERS OF MAMMALS). The two main groups of bats are the large fruit bats with a wing span of about 1m (see FRUIT BAT) and the small insect-eating bats with a wing span of about 30cm. The last group includes horseshoe bats with horseshoe-shaped nose-leaves*, simple-nosed bats, mastiff bats and many others (see GHOST BAT too). These small bats are sometimes called flitter-mice.

HOME: Bats are found in all warm parts of the world and all over Australia but are not often seen as they only fly at night and in warm weather. During the day and in cold weather they sleep hanging upside-down by their clawed hind feet in caves, in camps in thick forest or under the bark of trees. Females often gather in colonies in special caves to give birth to their young ones once a year. The baby is naked and blind but it hangs onto its mother's teat with its long teeth and is carried everywhere even when she flies about (see MAM-MAL-Placental). When it is older it stays behind in the cave while its mother hunts. All the young ones hang closely together on the cave roof, sometimes more than 1000 of them per square metre. When the females return each young bat hears the call of its own mother among the calls of the thousands of other bats.

FOOD: Bats mainly eat insects, fruit and blossoms.

Bush rat

KINDS: Bush rats are one group of native rats (see RAT). They belong to the Order Rodentia (see ORDERS OF MAMMALS). There are seven or eight kinds. Here are some of them.

SPECIES	COLOUR	HABITS
Southern*	brown/fluffy/tail and body same length	E. and S. coasts and islands/moist bush/ eats plants
Eastern swamp	brown/grey belly/ short tail	E. and S.E./swamps/ burrows/eats plants
Long-haired	grey or sandy/whitish belly/long hair!	dry inland/sometimes found in huge numbers
Tunney's	sandy/white belly/ short tail	northern half/grassland and sandy places

HOME: Bush rats are found in most parts of Australia but are rarely seen as they live deep in the bush and only move about at night. Some rats dig a burrow and make a nesting room at the end of it where the young are born, others make a nest under a log or among the roots of plants. In general, female bush rats have a litter (see WORDS) of 4 to 6 three or four times a year. The young are suckled for about 26 days (see MAMMAL—Placental). Most bush rats only live for about one year.

FOOD: Plants and seeds are the main foods eaten by bush rats, but, like other rats, they will eat almost anything if they are hungry.

GENERAL: Most bush rats are shy, furry, harmless animals unlike introduced rats (see INTRODUCED MAMMALS) but the dusky field-rat of Queensland damages cane crops and may carry disease.

Cuscus

KINDS: Cuscuses are related to brushtail possums (see POSSUM) although they look more like monkeys with their round heads, small ears and half-bare tails. They belong to the Order Marsupialia (see ORDERS OF MAMMALS). There are two species of cuscuses in Australia, the spotted cuscus* and the grey cuscus. The male (see WORDS) spotted cuscus has dark brown or grey fur blotched with large creamy spots. The female is usually plain coloured. Both male and female grey cuscuses have a dark stripe down the back.

HOME: Cuscuses are found in New Guinea and other islands in the Pacific Ocean as well as in the north-east of Australia on Cape York (see MAP). It is thought that they crossed to Australia from New Guinea a long, long time ago. They live in thick rain forests and dense scrub. During the day, a cuscus usually curls up and sleeps in the fork of a tree, but at night it moves around in the forest as it feeds. A female cuscus may have from 2 to 4 young ones at a time which she carries in her pouch (see MAMMAL—Marsupial).

FOOD: Cuscuses mainly eat leaves and fruit but sometimes they eat birds and other small animals.

GENERAL: Of all the possums, cuscuses are the largest in size but least is known about their way of life.
   The aborigines often caught and ate the slow moving cuscuses.

Dolphin

GENERAL: Dolphins are graceful, fast-swimming mammals which are sometimes seen playing in the waves at the bow of a boat or leaping out of the water as they swim along beside. But you can see dolphins in an aquarium too. There they are trained to jump through burning hoops, pull boats, ring bells and even play basketball! Dolphins seem to be at least as intelligent and as easily trained as dogs. They also seem to like to be with humans and although they have 88 to 200 teeth, the most of any mammal, they have never been known to bite or harm man in any way.

KINDS: There are about 50 species of dolphins with 3 or 4 kinds off Australian coasts. They belong to the Order Cetacea and to the group of toothed whales (see WHALE). A dolphin has silken smooth skin, cone-shaped teeth and a beak-like snout. Dolphins are often called porpoises but porpoises have spade-shaped teeth and no snout and are not seen in Australian waters. The common dolphin grows to about 2m and is black or brown with a white belly. The bottle-nosed dolphin* is the one most commonly seen in aquariums and grows to about 3.5m. Dolphins have very good hearing and guide themselves by echo-location like other whales (see WHALE and JUST FOR FUN). They also have good eyesight.

HOME: Dolphins live in all oceans. They move about in groups of from 10 to 1000. A young dolphin is born tail first then the mother pushes it up to the surface to breathe. It sucks milk from a gland near the mother's tail (see MAMMAL—Placental). Bottle-nosed dolphins have a habit of pushing anything which does not move, such as a sick dolphin or a log, up to the surface of the water.

FOOD: Dolphins mainly eat fish which they swallow head first.

Dugong

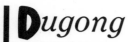

GENERAL: Have you ever seen a mermaid? You haven't?! Perhaps you have read about mermaids though, have you? They are mythical ladies with fish-tails who sit on rocks in the sea combing their long hair. Seamen of olden times told many tales about mermaids and it is thought that perhaps the dugong started off the tales. The female dugong often 'sits up' in the water with her young one clasped in her flippers so it can suckle. From a distance this can look like a person, then the 'person' may disappear with a flash of its fish-tail. Another tale tells of high sweet singing which lured sailors onto rocks. The 'singing' may have been made by a dugong because when a dugong's mate dies it often stays nearby for days afterwards loudly sighing and whistling every time it rises to breathe.

Unfortunately these interesting animals have been so hunted for their blubber and their hides that they are now rare and without further protection they could vanish.

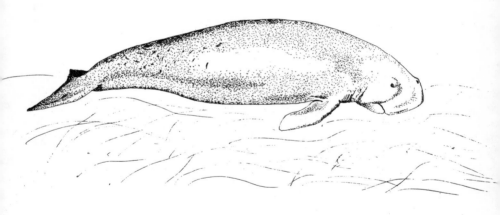

KINDS: The dugong is also called the sea-cow because it is slow, harmless and eats plants like a cow. It belongs to the Order Sirenia in which only a few living species (see WORDS) remain. The dugong has many fossilized ancestors and it is thought to be related to the elephant. The male dugong has small tusks like an elephant and the female has teats near her front legs like a female elephant. A dugong's nose looks like a squashed-in trunk too!

HOME: Dugongs are found around the northern part of Australia. They live in small herds in shallow bays and river mouths. When the single calf is born the mother suckles it and cares for it (see MAMMAL—Placental).

FOOD: Dugongs graze on sea grasses.

Dunnart

KINDS: Dunnarts are related to antechinuses (see ANTECHINUS) and are often called marsupial mice. They are mouse-sized and have soft fur and slender feet. There are at least 10 species (see WORDS) of dunnarts some of which are thin-tailed and some fat-tailed. A fat-tailed dunnart stores food in its tail which may become carrot-shaped when there is plenty of food around but thin when food is scarce. Here are a few species of dunnarts.

SPECIES	COLOUR	HABITS
Common	brown-grey/long thin tail/large ears/furry	S. and E./forests and swamps/burrows
Daly river	grey-brown/reddish cheeks/striped face	N. inland/forests/nests in logs or burrows
Fat-tailed*	grey-brown/dark patches on head/short tail	S. inland/scrub, grassland and stony places
Hairy-footed	fawn-white/long silver hairs on feet/big ears	desert C. and W./may be fat-tailed at times

HOME: Dunnarts are found in Australia and New Guinea. They live in most kinds of country from deserts to rain forests. Usually a dunnart makes a grass nest in a hollow log or in a burrow in the ground where it sleeps all day. The female may have a litter (see WORDS) of 10 three or four times a year. The young live in the pouch, then when they are bigger are carried around hanging onto the mother's fur (see MAMMAL—Marsupial).

FOOD: Dunnarts eat insects, spiders, lizards, mice and other small animals.

GENERAL: Some dunnarts become torpid (see WORDS) each day or when food is scarce in order to save their energy.

Dunnarts are fearless little animals and will threaten attackers with wide-open mouths and noisy hisses.

Euro

KINDS: Another name for a euro is a wallaroo. Both names come from aboriginal names. Euros are the kind of kangaroos (see KANGAROO) which live among rocks. A euro has long, broad hind feet, often with roughened soles which help it grip on smooth rock. It has a bare muzzle (see WORDS) like a dog and is more solidly built than a kangaroo. Some euros have shaggy, dark grey fur, some have shorter red-brown fur and others are fawn coloured. The female is often paler than the male. Male euros may be large and heavy and can be dangerous if cornered.

HOME: Euros are found only in Australia. They live in barren ranges, rugged mountains and on rocky ridges. They usually move about in small groups made up of one male or 'old man', several females or does and joeys of various ages, but sometimes an 'old man' lives alone. The female euro usually has one joey each year (see MAMMAL—Marsupial) but if there is little food she may not breed (see WORDS).

FOOD: Euros eat grass and plants. When food is scarce the euro, like the quokka (see QUOKKA), is able to re-use some of its own body wastes to help keep it alive. It is also able to live for long periods without water if necessary.

GENERAL: A euro stands upright with its hands held close to its body when it jumps along. When it is frightened it does not stop and look back to see what has frightened it as do other kangaroos.

Fruit bat

KINDS: Fruit bats are often called flying foxes and although their faces do look 'foxy' they are bats that eat fruit, not foxes which fly, but they are known by both names. Most fruit bats weigh about 1 kg and have a wing span of about 1 m. They are one group of bats (see BAT) and belong to the Order Chiroptera (say—ki/rop/tra). There are about 82 species (see WORDS) with four species in Australia. Here they are:

SPECIES	COLOUR	HABITS
Grey-headed* (colour photo 14)	grey/wide rust collar furry—even on legs	E. coast/may eat fruit in orchards
Little reddish	reddish all over/paler head/narrow ears	coasts of N. half/ eats gum blossoms
Black	black-brown all over/ paler collar	N. coasts/mangroves/ will bite/eats fruit
Spectacled	grey-brown/yellow 'spectacles'	rain forests/N.E./ often with black species

HOME: Fruit bats live in the warm parts of India, south-east Asia, Australia and islands of the Pacific. They fly about and feed at night. In the daytime they gather in huge numbers in 'camps' in thick forest to sleep hanging upside-down. The camps are often noisy because the bats not only sleep but also bicker and quarrel. Usually the female bat gives birth to one young one each year (see MAMMAL—Placental) which is carried around hanging onto its mother's teat until it is weaned at about four months.

FOOD: With their broad flat teeth fruit bats pulp up the fruit and blossoms which they eat.

GENERAL: Fruit bats have good sight and guide themselves much more with their eyes when they are flying than do other bats.
They probably find their food by smell.

Ghost bat

KINDS: Another name for the ghost bat is the false vampire bat. It belongs to the group of insect-eating bats (see BAT) and like all other bats in Australia, is harmless to man. Most ghost bats are pale ashy-grey and have large 'ghostly' wings.They have erect nose-leaves, large eyes, large ears joined together in the middle, no tails and no teeth at the top at the front. They guide themselves through the darkness like many other bats by beaming out ultrasonic sounds and then listening to the echoes that return to them. They may look 'ugly' to us but they possess an extra radar sense that we might envy!

HOME: Ghost bats are now only found in the northern half of Australia. Thick layers of their droppings have been found in caves in the south but the bats no longer live there. Usually they roost in caves, deserted mines or wells but they are so ghost-like in their movements that often it is difficult to see them even if you are looking for them! About November each year the females (see WORDS) gather in colonies to give birth to their young ones (see MAMMAL—Placental).

FOOD: Ghost bats eat lizards, birds, insects, mice, rats and other bats. They drop down over their prey with their wings and kill it by biting it on the head. They eat all of the animal even the bones, fur, teeth and small feathers.

GENERAL: Young ghost bats are dark grey and some adults in the far north of Australia are also dark grey.

Glider possum

GENERAL: A glider possum can only glide downwards, it cannot fly in the way a bat or a bird can. It has loose folds of skin along the sides of its body which are stretched out by the legs into an oblong shape when the possum glides*. The long furry tail acts as a balancer. Large possums have been seen to cover more than 100m in one glide.

KINDS: There are about 5 species of glider possums in the possum family (see POSSUM). Each glider possum is more closely related to a non-gliding possum than it is to another glider. The feather-tail glider is related to the pigmy possums and the greater glider to the ringtails (see RINGTAIL POSSUM).

SPECIES	LENGTH/COLOUR	HABITS
Squirrel	50cm total/grey-fawn/ stripe/cream belly	E./forests/eats insects, sap and flowers/rare
Feather-tail (colour photo 12) (* below)	called 'flying mouse'/ brown/white belly	E. and S.E./gum trees/ groups/rarely seen
Fluffy	75cm total/grey-brown- black/yellow belly	E. coast/mountains/ calls as it glides
Greater or dusky*	largest/tail 50cm/grey- black/white belly	E./tall trees/eats gum leaves

See SUGAR GLIDER too

FOOD: Most glider possums eat leaves, blossoms and insects.

HOME: Glider possums are found in the east of Australia only and in New Guinea. They live in thick bushland and sleep all day in a nest of gum leaves or twigs in a hole in a tree. The feather-tail and the sugar glider live in groups but other gliders live alone or in pairs. Most of the time the female (see WORDS) has one or two young ones in her pouch (see MAMMAL— Marsupial).

Hare wallaby

KINDS: Hare wallabies are the smallest kind of wallaby (see WALLABY). They are about the size of a hare and can move as fast as a hare. Mostly they have a ring of orange hairs around the eye but this is brighter in some species than in others. All except the banded hare wallaby have hairy muzzles (see WORDS). There are 4 species. Here they are.

SPECIES	COLOUR	HABITS
Banded	grey/dark bands across back/bare muzzle	S.W. and islands/thick scrub/lives in groups
Spectacled	brown-buff/bright orange 'spectacles'	N. and C./rare now/ grasslands/solitary
Brown*	brown!/black on elbow/slender	E. inland/very rare now/ tame/very fast
Western	brownish/long reddish hair on lower back	C. and W., islands/once common/spinifex/ burrows

HOME: Hare wallabies were once common in Australia. They are now only found in any numbers on islands off the south and west coasts. They have probably become rare because sheep and cattle grazing changed their living places and introduced foxes and cats preyed on them. Usually a hare wallaby lives alone. It makes a 'hide', the same as a hare, under a clump of grass or in an open-ended burrow where it sleeps all day. The female (see WORDS) carries one joey in her pouch at a time (see MAMMAL—Marsupial).

FOOD: Hare wallabies eat grass and plants.

GENERAL: If a hare wallaby is chased it can run for a long time at high speed and make leaps of up to 2m high.

Honey possum

FOOD: The honey possum mainly eats pollen and nectar from native flowers such as bottlebrush and gum. It has a long snout which fits into flowers and a brush-like tongue to sweep up the pollen. Its lips can be curled into a tube-shape for sucking up nectar. Its teeth are only small because most of its food does not have to be chewed but it is thought that it may sometimes eat the soft parts of insects which it finds among the flowers.

KINDS: The honey possum* belongs to the Order Marsupialia (see ORDERS OF MAMMALS) but it is not closely related to any known living animal. It is the size of a mouse and looks something like a pigmy possum (see POSSUM) with three dark stripes down its back. A honey possum scampers around on the ground, in shrubs and in trees, often using its tail to hang by. The aboriginal name for the honey possum is the noolbenger.

HOME: The south-west corner of Western Australia is the only place where the honey possum is found. It is still fairly common there but it could easily vanish if more of its living places were taken over for farming. It lives in pairs or small groups among flowering trees and shrubs moving about wherever the flowers are most plentiful. It makes a small round nest of grass and fur in a low shrub where the young ones live when they move out of their mother's pouch (see MAMMAL—Marsupial) at about four months of age. The female is bigger than the male and usually has twins each year.

GENERAL: Like the pigmy possum, a honey possum sleeps all day with its head between its front paws and its tail forward up over its head.

Hopping mouse

KINDS: Hopping mice are one group of native mice (see MOUSE) and belong to the Order Rodentia (see ORDERS OF MAMMALS). Hopping mice are about 30cm long overall with the head and body 12-14cm (how long is the tail?). The ears may be 2.5cm long and the feet 4cm long. Most hopping mice have a patch of long hair or a tiny pouch filled with long hair on their neck or chest which is thought to be a scent gland. There are at least 9 species of hopping mice. Here are a few of them.

SPECIES	COLOUR	HABITS
Mitchell's	sandy-brown/long white hairs on chest	S.inland/first seen by explorer Mitchell in 1836
Dusky*	brown/deep neck pouch	arid inland/may jump 3m
Long tailed	yellow-brown/small ears/rat-sized	C. Inland/burrows in stiff clayey soil
Spinifex (colour photo 3)	sandy/neck pouch	C./deserts/fast digger

HOME: Hopping mice are found in most parts of Australia except along the east coast. Many live in hot, dry places among grass or trees, or in sandy desert country. They dig tunnels about 2cm across which go straight down for 30cm, then straight across and straight down again to the nesting room about 1m underground. They also dig several escape tunnels. The female usually has a litter (see WORDS) of 4-6 several times a year.

FOOD: Hopping mice eat plants, seeds and berries. Some kinds are able to live without water for long periods but they will drink if water is available.

GENERAL: Hopping mice sleep in their burrows all day and feed at night. In a good season in some places there are hundreds of hopping mice but when there is little food they all seem to disappear.

Introduced mammals

You know what dogs and cats look like, don't you? You have probably seen horses, sheep and other farm animals too. These common mammals are not native to Australia, they have been introduced or brought in from other countries. Most introduced farm mammals are useful to us although in some places they have been kept in such large numbers that they have damaged the land. Other introduced mammals such as pigs, goats, buffaloes, foxes and cats have gone wild and become pests (see WORDS) and pushed many native mammals out of their living places. Here are a few.

DINGO*: The dingo is often thought of as a native mammal because it came to Australia a long, long time ago, probably with the aborigines when they crossed to Australia from Asia. It looks like a large goldy-coloured dog but it makes a howling sound unlike any other dog or wolf. Dingoes are easily tamed but often they live in the wild and hunt in packs sometimes killing sheep. Because of this, large numbers of dingoes have been shot and many fences have been erected in an attempt to keep sheep safe from dingo attacks.

FOX: The European fox was brought into Australia about 1868 so that people could go fox-hunting as they did in Britain. As a result of this introduction, the fox has become one of the worst pests in Australia. It kills hens, lambs and many native mammals and birds for food. It is smaller than a dog and has reddish fur and a bushy tail.

HARE: The introduced hare is bigger and runs faster than a rabbit but it does not breed (see WORDS) as rapidly. It eats grass but is not such a pest as the rabbit (see below).

MOUSE: The introduced mouse is now a pest all over Australia. It breeds (see WORDS) very quickly. Mice live in houses and sheds as well as in the bush and the dry inland. Mice might even live in your house and if they do you will know that they run about at night gnawing at things, eating food scraps and leaving their droppings everywhere. They look very much like native mice (see MOUSE) except that the female has ten teats instead of four.

RABBIT: Rabbits are cuddly-looking little animals with long ears, soft fur and fluffy tails, but unfortunately they are one of the worst pests that has ever been introduced into Australia. One pair of rabbits will multiply, even if half of them die, into over 70 000 in two years! Rabbits eat the grass which sheep and native mammals live on, they make long burrows which cause the ground to collapse into wash-outs, they ring-bark trees and have pushed many native mammals out of their living places.

RAT: The two species of introduced rats are both pests. The long-tailed ship rat is grey, brown or dusky black. It has large ears and short fur. It is now found all over Australia and often lives in houses and storage sheds where it causes much damage. The sewer rat is grey, reddish-brown or black. It has large strong feet, a short thick tail and coarse thin fur. It usually lives in cities in drains, under floors and in sewers. It will eat anything even other sick rats and garbage. Both these introduced rats may be carriers of a number of horrible diseases to man, so make sure that introduced rats do not live at your place! The female sewer rat may have a litter of more than 10 young ones every month of the year. If none died, one pair of rats would multiply to 350 million rats in three years! The number of rats in the story about the Pied Piper of Hamelin could easily be true!

Just for fun

ABILITIES: Mammals are able to learn more things than any other group of animals. Apes have been taught to do many things such as clean their teeth, get dressed and talk in deaf and dumb language. Dolphins (see DOLPHIN) and dogs, mice and rats, horses and pigs and other mammals can also be taught to do simple things. And what about you?! You can read this book, a very clever mammal! Humans are classed physically with the mammals but mentally they are very different from every other animal. Could your dog ever learn to read this page? Or play football? Or tell you a story? Humans are different because they are aware of themselves and of others, they have imagination and the mental ability to build cities and cars, to move hills and rivers, to fly to the moon and do many other incredible things. Humans can change their surroundings and their living places in any way they like to suit themselves which is something that no other animal can do. But because humans are able to do this they must be careful that in the process they do not endanger or kill themselves and the other living things on which their lives depend. (see UP TO YOU).

AGES: The *longest-living land mammal* after humans is the Asiatic elephant which may live for 70 years. Kangaroos, whales and bats live about 20 years. Some small animals like shrews and some rats live about one year.

BLUE WHALE: The largest and heaviest animal that has ever lived in the world and still lives today is the blue whale (see WHALE). The longest blue whale accurately recorded was 33.58m. The heaviest weighed 177 tonnes. An average blue whale of about 130 tonnes weighs as much as 4 bronto-sauruses or 25 elephants or 150 cows or 1 600 people! A blue whale's tongue weighs almost as much as an elephant. When a blue whale is born it weighs about 3 tonnes and is 6m long. When it is seven months old and about 23 tonnes in weight it is weaned (see WORDS).

EARS: Many mammals, particularly those active at night, have very good hearing and large outer ears which can be moved in any direction to pick up sounds. Most mammals can hear much higher sounds than the ones we can hear.

ECHO LOCATION: Some mammals guide themselves through darkness in the air at night or underwater or underground by using echo location (see BAT and WHALE). It is thought that the ultrasonic clicks beamed out by whales and dolphins are forced out through a special part of the forehead. As the outer ear holes are closed underwater, it seems that, in the dolphin at least, echoes from objects are received through some of the head bones and then passed to the inner ear.

EYES: Most mammals have good eyesight and some can see quite well in dim light. Your cat and other nocturnal (see WORDS) mammals have a reflector or tapetum behind their eyes which helps them to see in dim light. These mammals also often have slit pupils in their eyes, unlike the round ones in yours, which protect their eyes in the daytime by keeping out more light.

NUMBERS: There are about 5000 known species of mammals with 250 in Australia. About 250 species are marsupials with about 150 of them in Australia.

RECORDS:
Largest marsupial mammal—kangaroo/Australia/tallest—2.7m—red kangaroo*/heaviest—over 90kg—grey kangaroo.
Smallest marsupial mammal—flat-skulled planigale/Australia/length—body 4.4cm—tail 5cm/weight about 4g.
Largest living land mammal—bush elephant/Africa/about 3.2m tall/weight about 5 tonnes.
Deepest depth to which a whale has dived—3193m by a sperm whale/the same whale stayed under water for 1 hour 52 minutes.

Kangaroo

GENERAL: An aboriginal legend tells how Kangaroo-man always slept outside under the stars and Wombat-man slept in a cosy hut he had built for himself. One wet windy night Kangaroo-man began to think longingly about Wombat-man's hut. At last when he was very wet and miserable he went and knocked on the door. Wombat-man let him in but made him stand by the draughty door all night while Wombat-man snored away in front of the fire. By the morning Kangaroo-man was so cross that he hit Wombat-man on the head with a rock, flattening his skull, so then Wombat-man threw a spear into Kangaroo-man's bottom and there it has been ever since as a long tail.

A kangaroo does have a long tail as you probably know! It is used for steering when a kangaroo is hopping quickly on its hind legs and as an extra leg when the kangaroo is moving slowly along on four legs to graze (colour photo 9).

The male (see WORDS) kangaroo is often called an 'old man' or a 'boomer'. It grows all its life and many 'old men' are over 2m tall and over 80kg in weight. The female or doe is much smaller and often only weighs 30kg (see JUST FOR FUN—Records too).

A kangaroo usually bounds along covering 1-2m with each hop, but when it is in a hurry each hop may be longer. It can jump over things 1-2m high. If an 'old man' is chased by dogs it may leap into water and then drown the dogs one by one as they attack.

Adult male kangaroos can be very dangerous if cornered, but mostly kangaroos are gentle, harmless animals. They are inquisitive too and when they are alarmed they often stop and look behind to see what has frightened them. This habit makes kangaroos easy to shoot and in some places they are shot in large numbers for pet food, for their skins or because they are pests. Some shooting of kangaroos may be necessary at times but it must always be controlled so that this unique and gentle animal does not vanish.

KINDS: Marsupial mammals which eat grass and have long hind feet belong to the kangaroo or large-footed family (see ORDERS OF MAMMALS). Kangaroos are the largest members of the family with the hind foot longer than 25cm (see WALLABY). Like some other marsupials they have a combing toe on this foot (see BANDICOOT). There are three main kinds of kangaroos— grey kangaroos, red kangaroos and euros or wallaroos (see EURO). The female red kangaroo is often smoky-blue in colour and is sometimes called the 'blue flyer'. When you see a large kangaroo you can tell which kind it is by first looking at its colour and then at its muzzle (see WORDS). The muzzle of a grey kangaroo is completely covered with hair; a red kangaroo's is half covered with hair and a euro's is bare like a dog's (look at the drawings below). The picture above is of a grey kangaroo. Its muzzle is covered with hair.

HOME: Kangaroos are found only in Australia where they live in most places. Grey kangaroos live in forests in the east and in the south-west corner. Red kangaroos live on the inland plains and euros live among rocks (see EURO). A female kangaroo has a forward opening pouch in which she usually has a joey (colour photos 10 and 11). When one joey leaves the pouch at about 8 months of age another one is born (see MAMMAL— Marsupial). In dry seasons few joeys survive but in good times a female may rear four joeys in three years.

FOOD: Kangaroos eat grass and other plants. Scientists have found that usually sheep and kangaroos eat different kinds of grass.

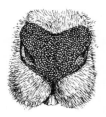

Grey Kangaroo   Red Kangaroo   Euro

Koala

HOME: Koalas are found only in Australia. They are now quite rare and mostly only live in parks and sanctuaries. One hundred and fifty years ago koalas were common in the forests of New South Wales, Victoria, Queensland and South Australia but many were killed for their fur and many died from diseases and the koala almost vanished. Luckily in the 1930's some sanctuaries and parks were set aside especially for koalas and people began to study their lives and habits.

1   Young spiny anteater

2   Adult spiny anteater

3 Spinifex hopping mouse

4 Antechinus showing teeth

5 Kultarr

In general, the female (see WORDS) koala gives birth to one young about every second year. At birth the young one looks something like a fat worm about 2cm long and weighs 5½g (see MAMMAL—Marsupial). It crawls into its mother's pouch and stays there for 5 or 6 months. When it comes out for the first time it is a quaint, furry little animal about 18cm long. It uses the pouch for another two months and then it is carried around on its mother's back or in her arms until it is about one year old. When it is four years old it is fully grown and it may live until it is twenty.

KINDS: There is only one species of koala which belongs in a family (see WORDS) of its own in the Order Marsupialia (see ORDERS OF MAMMALS). A koala is grey and white. It has fluffy ears, a bare button nose and often appears to have a surprised look on its face*. It is known around the world as Australia's 'teddy-bear' but it is not really a bear at all! Although it lives most of its life in trees, it seems to be more closely related to the wombat (see WOMBAT) than to any other animal. Like the wombat it has a backward opening pouch for its young with two teats in it, cheek pouches and no tail. A koala usually sleeps curled up in the fork of a tree all day and feeds and moves around at night when it climbs easily about gripping the tree trunk with its sharp claws. It is a slow-moving, harmless animal.

FOOD: Koalas only eat eucalyptus or gum leaves, which means they would not be able to live in many other countries of the world would they? A koala eats more than 1kg of leaves each day. If you picked a kilo of leaves you would see what a big mound it is! The koala will eat leaves from about 12 species of gum trees but at certain times of the year, the young leaves contain a poison which will kill the animal, so the koala must have plenty of trees to choose from so it can avoid the poisonous leaves. Occasionally a koala will eat some dirt but it rarely drinks water. One aboriginal legend tells about a koala which stole coolamons (containers) of water and hid them up a tree because the tribe would not give him any water to drink. Finally the aborigines got their coolamons of water back and punished the koala and ever since then he has eaten gum leaves which give him both food and water, but he is still waiting for the day to steal the water from the aborigines again! The word 'koala' comes from the aboriginal word which means 'no drink'. The cheek pouches inside a koala's mouth help it to hold and chew its bulky food. In its gut is a special 'appendix', 1 or 2m long, which helps digest the chewed up gum leaves.

GENERAL: A koala makes a grunting sound like a pig but if it is hurt or upset it makes a wailing sound. A young one may cry like a baby.

Koalas are one of Australia's unique animals and are of interest to all people. It is up to us to see that they are protected and that they do not vanish. But even so, in 1988 it was estimated that there are only about 400,000 koalas left in Australia and of this number, almost half are suffering from some disease. Our koalas need immediate help or they could really die out this time.

Kultarr

KINDS: Kultarrs are small marsupials related to dunnarts (see DUNNART) and belong to the native cat family (see ORDERS OF MAMMALS). They are often called jerboas but true jerboas of other countries hop about and are rodents (see RAT) not marsupials. Kultarrs gallop about using their tails as rudders. There is only one species and it is quite rare. A kultarr is about the size of a mouse and has long hind legs and a tuft of hairs on the end of its tail. It has large ears and only four toes on its long hind foot* (colour photo 5).

HOME: The kultarr is found only in Australia. It lives in the dry inland parts of the east, centre and west. It sometimes digs its own burrow with only one entrance, but often it uses the burrow of a mouse. The female kultarr has a flap-like pouch which opens backwards with six teats (see WORDS) in it. A female has been caught with six young ones in her pouch (see MAMMAL —Marsupial) but very little is known about the habits of this little animal.

FOOD: Kultarrs, like dunnarts and antechinuses have a number of teeth at the front. They eat insects and other small animals.

GENERAL: A kultarr sleeps in its burrow all day where it is cool and comes out to feed at night.

Kultarrs and hopping mice often live in the same places and look quite alike. Can you list the differences between them? Start with pouch and look up HOPPING MOUSE to help you.

Long-eared bat

KINDS: Long-eared bats are one group of insect-eating bats (see BAT). Like ghost bats (see GHOST BAT) they have large ears joined together in the middle above the forehead which are folded down tightly when the bat sleeps. They only have a ridge on their nose and probably send out their echo location sounds through the mouth. Most long-eared bats are ashy-grey or brown in colour. There are 4 or 5 kinds.

SPECIES	SIZE	HABITS
Greater	body 10cm long/ear 2.5cm/hairy nose	E., S. and S.W./ trees and caves
Lesser* (colour photo 13)	body 8cm/slender ear 2cm/high nose ridge	southern half/common/ caves, trees, houses
North Queensland	smaller than greater species	houses and trees/ rich brown colour
Arnhem land	smaller than lesser species/ear 2cm	North/lives under bark

HOME: Long-eared bats are found in many countries and in most of Australia except the arid centre. They usually roost in tree holes, under bark or in caves and rock crevices. They live in small colonies of males and females (see WORDS). Usually the female gives birth to twins once a year which are carried around for some time hanging onto the teats under the mother's arms (see MAMMAL—Placental).

FOOD: Long-eared bats eat insects and sometimes land on the ground to pick them up.

GENERAL: Little is known about the movements of long-eared bats or other bats in Australia. Under the Bat-Banding Scheme numbers of bats have been banded in the hope of finding out more about their habits but so far, few of the banded bats have been recaptured.

29

Mammal

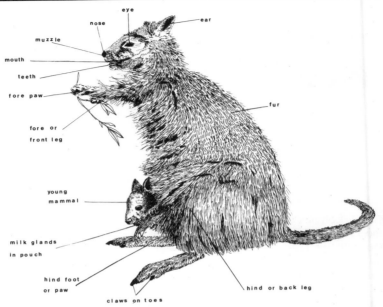

eye
nose
ear
muzzle
mouth
teeth
fore paw
fur
fore or
front leg
young
mammal
milk glands
in pouch
hind foot
or paw
hind or back leg
claws on toes

Mammals are one class of animals. Birds are also a class and so are insects. Can you think of another class? (Fish, spiders. What else?) Scientists group animals into classes by the way their bodies look from both inside and outside and by their habits. A wallaby*, a tiger, a mouse and a whale are all mammals. You are a mammal too and so is your dog! Animals in the same class always have some physical or bodily features in common. Here is a list of features that most mammals have.

A MAMMAL usually *has fur or hair* on all or parts of its body; *gives birth to live young*, that is, it does not lay eggs except for the platypus and spiny anteater; *suckles its young on milk* from its milk glands. (The word 'mammal' comes from the Latin word *mamma* meaning breast or milk gland); *breathes air with lungs*, not gills like a fish; *has a backbone*; mostly *has teeth of 4 different shapes* for biting and chewing; *is warm-blooded* with a body temperature between 36°C and 39°C all the time, except for the platypus (30.8°C) and the spiny anteater (29.9°C); *has a large front part of the brain* which enables it to learn more things than any other animal.

Well, you are a mammal aren't you? But a very special one I think! (See JUST FOR FUN—Abilities)

Mammals are divided into three main groups based on the stages at which the young are born. They are: 1) Monotreme—all mammals in the Order Monotremata (see ORDERS OF MAMMALS) 2) Marsupial—all mammals in the Order Marsupialia 3) Placental—all other mammals. This table shows you the stage at which the young of each group is born and how the young develops.

MONOTREME	MARSUPIAL	PLACENTAL
egg-laying mammals platypus, spiny anteater *only* egg laid in nest or pouch/young hatches/looks unlike adult	pouched mammals/ wombat, kangaroo, possum etc.	most mammals/young is joined to mother by placental or navel cord

| young suckles/ grows | young is born/unlike adult/crawls into pouch | |

| suckles/grows | attaches to teat/ suckles/grows | young is born/quite like adult/suckles |

| leaves nest/grows | suckles/grows | suckles/grows |

| grows/becomes adult | leaves pouch/grows/ becomes adult | leaves nest/grows/ becomes adult |

31

Mole

KINDS: The marsupial mole was first described in 1888. It looks like the golden mole of South Africa but the Australian mole is a marsupial (see MAMMAL) and seems to have no relatives. It is the only species in a family of its own. The marsupial mole is about 15cm long and covered with fine silky golden-yellow fur. It has a horny cover over its nose, long thick claws and a short cone-shaped tail. It has only a small hole for an ear and seems to have no eyes at all. The next time you think of telling someone they are as 'blind as a bat', make it better and tell them they are as 'blind as a mole'!

HOME: The marsupial mole is found only in Australia. It lives in sandy desert country in the inland. It moves around in the soil about 7cm under the surface, then comes up and wriggles along on top of the soil for a while before burrowing in again. Little is known about the mole but it is thought that the female may make a burrow with a nest in it for her young (see MAMMAL—Marsupial).

FOOD: Moles probably eat ants, beetle larvae and other small animals which live in the soil.

GENERAL: A mole makes a low squeaking or chirping sound.
    Not many moles have been caught but one which was kept in a box for a while had bursts of activity. It would wake up, shuffle around at top speed, eat its food at top speed and then suddenly fall asleep.

ouse

KINDS: The mouse that runs out of your cupboard or nibbles food in your kitchen is probably the introduced mouse (see INTRODUCED MAMMALS). In Australia there are also about 20 species of native mice which look like the introduced mouse and are also rodents (see RAT), but unlike the introduced mouse, most native mice have soft fur and big ears and the female has only four teats (see WORDS). Most mice have a head and body about 12cm long. Here are a few kinds.

SPECIES	COLOUR/SIZE	HABITS
Pebble mound	yellow-brown/white belly/medium size	common/C./grassy and stony hills/burrows in pebbles
Delicate	greyish-fawn/white belly/tiny	N. half/makes grass nest in a shallow burrow
Grey	silvery/medium	S. half/burrows/sandhills
New Holland*	grey-brown/medium	eastern N.S.W./rare
Eastern	brown/ears 2cm/large	grassy plains/burrows

See HOPPING MOUSE too

HOME: Mice are found all over Australia but they are rarely seen as they run about at night and live far away from houses in the bush and in deserts. Most female mice have a litter (see WORDS) every few months (see MAMMAL—Placental).

FOOD: Mice eat plants, bark, seeds and many other things. Constant gnawing makes their teeth very sharp.

GENERAL: Little is known about the native mice of Australia although a few species have been studied. It is thought that overall their numbers have probably decreased since white settlement.

Native cat

KINDS: Your cat is not related to the native cats. To make this plain, native cats are now sometimes called *Dasyurus* or quolls. Native cats are related to Tasmanian devils, antechinuses and other meat-eating marsupials (see MAMMAL). There are four species. Once upon a time, so the aboriginal legend says, there was a Cat-man who ate women and children. When the tribesmen finally killed him he turned into a brown animal the size of a cat with white spots on him showing where each spear had pierced him.

SPECIES	COLOUR/SIZE	HABITS
Eastern or quoll (colour photo 15)	brown/no spots on tail but may have white tip	E.bushland/once common/eats mice, rats, birds
Western or chuditch	brown/no spots on tail	inland and S.W./may live on ground and in trees
Tiger cat*	brown-yellow/white spots on tail/large	common Tas./rare now in E./forests/tree dweller
Little northern or satanellus	yellow-brown/no spots on tail/small	N./logs and rocks/colour varies/solitary

HOME: Native cats are found only in Australia. They were once common but are now rare except in Tasmania. Numbers were killed because they ate farm chickens and many died from disease. They climb easily and mostly live in trees. A female native cat develops a pouch before the young ones are born. There may be six young in a litter (see WORDS). When they are too big for the pouch they are carried about hanging onto the mother's fur.

FOOD: Native cats mostly eat birds, rats, mice, rabbits, insects, lizards and other small animals.

GENERAL: Native cats sleep all day. At night they are fearless and often ferocious hunters.

34

Numbat

HOME: The numbat or banded anteater is another Australian mammal which could vanish unless the remaining forests of wandoo gum where it lives are preserved. Many of these forests have been cleared for settlement so the living places of the numbat have shrunk. Once it was fairly common in much of the south but now it is only found in the south-west corner of Western Australia. The numbat usually makes a nest in a hollow log where it sleeps all night. It is thought that some females make a short nesting burrow for their 3 or 4 young ones. When the young are very tiny the mother carries them around attached to her teats. Although the numbat has no pouch it is a marsupial because of the stage at which the young are born (see MAMMAL—Marsupial).

KINDS: The numbat is not closely related to any other known mammal and it is the only species in a family of its own (see ORDERS OF MAMMALS). It is a pretty little animal about 45cm long with reddish-brown fur banded white across the back*. A numbat often frisks about holding up its tail in the air like a large bottlebrush.

FOOD: Numbats mainly eat termites or 'white ants' as they are commonly called. They scratch among the forest litter (see WORDS) and lap up the termites they find usually swallowing them whole although numbats have about 50 small teeth.

GENERAL: Numbats are not afraid of people and are often quite easy to see in the daytime in the State forests near Perth, W.A.

A numbat may trot about on the ground then leap from log to log and sometimes climb a tree or a stump. It may make a 'tut-tutting' sound as it scampers around. It is a gentle harmless animal.

Orders of mammals

Over hundreds of years scientists have arranged and grouped all known animals into a system to show their relationships. The animals are known by the same scientific or Latinized (see WORDS) name around the world. Usually they also have common names which often vary from place to place. Common names are mainly used in this book. Scientists put distantly related animals into a Class. More closely related animals, such as all those mammals with pouches, are put in the same Order, while families and species show even closer relationships. In the Class of mammals there are about 18 Orders with mammals in 7 Orders living in or around Australia. Here is a diagram showing you the relationships of the land mammals in the 4 Orders found in Australia. A diagram of world mammals would be very large with the 18 Orders in it and with different families added to 3 of the Orders shown here. Which Order would not be added to because it is uniquely Australian? (See ANTEATER—SPINY)

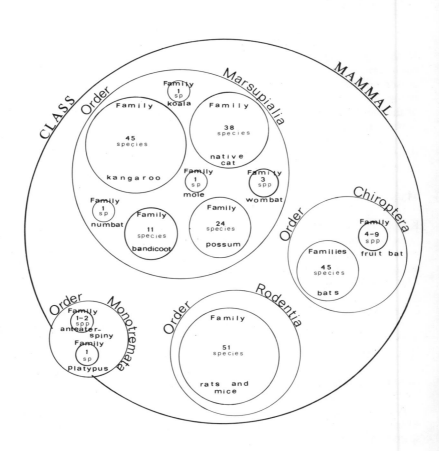

Pademelon

KINDS: Small wallabies (see WALLABY) are often called by the part-aboriginal name 'pademelon'. A pademelon is a harmless, gentle little animal with each hind foot less than 15cm long. It has a short thick tail and when it sits up on its hind legs it is about 1m tall. Females are smaller than males (see WORDS). There are 5 or 6 species of pademelons or small wallabies.

SPECIES	COLOUR	HABITS
Red-necked (colour photo 6)	brownish-grey/reddish neck/pale belly	coastal N.S.W. and south Q./common in places
Red-legged	brown-red/reddish legs/ pale yellow hip stripe	rain forests/N.S.W. and Q./now rare in many places
Red-bellied*	dark brown/red belly/ small ears/shaggy	common in Tas./lives in large groups
Tammar (colour photo 7)	greyish-brown/reddish shoulders	S. coasts and islands/can live in very dry places

See QUOKKA too.

HOME: Pademelons were once common over much of the east and south of Australia but some species are now rare. They live in thick scrub or tangled grass, often beside swamps, in which they make tunnel-like runways. They move out of the runways to feed but at any disturbance they flee back into them. Usually the female pademelons have one joey each year (see MAMMAL—Marsupial).

FOOD: Pademelons eat grass, leaves and shoots.

GENERAL: By studying tammars it has been found that they obtain most of the water they need from their food. This enables them to live in dry places. Wheat farming has taken over much of the tammar or casuarina scrub country where the tammar lives in the south-west of W.A. so its living place is shrinking. What could this mean for this mammal? (Hint—see VANISHING ANIMALS)

Platypus

KINDS: When the first platypus skin was sent to England in 1802, scientists thought that someone had played a joke on them by stitching together parts of two or three different animals. Whoever heard of an animal with a beak like a duck, a furry body like a cat, webbed feet with claws like an otter and a broad flat tail shaped like a beaver's but furry, not bare! Then in 1824 it was found that the platypus fed its young on milk and in 1884 it was proved that it laid eggs like a snake or a bird! It also breathes air like you do but lives a lot of the time in water like a fish! Puzzle—what sort of an animal is it? It was quite a long time before scientists agreed about that! They finally decided to class it as a mammal (see MAMMAL). It was put into an Order with the other egg-laying mammal, the spiny anteater (see ANTEATER—SPINY) in a family of its own (see ORDERS OF MAMMALS). It was given the scientific name of *Ornithorhynchus anatinus* which tells us it has a duck-like snout.

An adult platypus* has a body about 45cm long and a tail of 15cm. It may weigh 1 or 2kg. It is covered with thick brown fur on all but the belly where it is whitish. Its duck-like snout is not hard like a bird's beak but is soft and leathery and is used for feeling with, something like your fingers (colour photo 16).

HOME: The platypus is found only in Australia and only in the eastern quarter. It lives in any quiet fresh-water creek or lake in mountains or on the plains. It digs two burrows. One is a short 'living-room', often under the roots of a tree and with two entrances. The other is a nesting burrow and is dug by the female (see WORDS). The entrance may be 1-3m above the water and the burrow is sometimes 18m long. At the end of the burrow the female makes a nest of grass, leaves and twigs*. When she is ready to lay her eggs she puts walls of mud across the burrow at intervals so that no water or enemies can get in. She lays two large soft-shelled eggs and nurses them for 10 days. When the young hatch they suck milk from the mother's milk glands. They stay in the nest for about six weeks and are ready for their first swim when they are about four months old (see MAMMAL—Monotreme).

FOOD: The platypus has a huge appetite and eats almost its own weight in food every day. When it dives under water a fold of skin covers its ears and eyes. It finds its food by feeling about in the mud and slush in the bottom of the water with its leathery snout. It eats insect larvae, worms, tadpoles, small prawns and other small water animals. It holds the food in the pouches in its cheeks then rises to the surface to chew and swallow it. The platypus can stay under water for about one minute. It usually feeds early in the morning and again in the evening.

GENERAL: The male platypus has poison spurs on its hind legs which can cause a painful wound in humans and may kill a dog. But in the main the platypus is a harmless and unique animal.

Like most other native mammals, the platypus is protected by law but so as to make sure it does survive we must take care not to pollute or disturb any waterways where it lives.

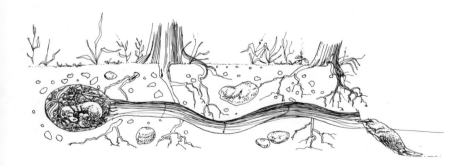

Possum

KINDS: There are six or seven groups of possums in Australia all of which belong to the possum family in the Order Marsupialia (see ORDERS OF MAMMALS). These pages tell you something about pigmy possums, brushtail possums and the striped possum. For other possums look up CUSCUS, GLIDER POSSUM, HONEY POSSUM, RINGTAIL POSSUM and VANISHING MAMMALS.

Possums have thick fur and long tails which are used for gripping and balancing and sometimes for carrying twigs and leaves to the nest. They have sharp claws on their hand-like paws which enable them to climb easily. Like some other marsupials they have a combing toe on each hind foot (see KANGAROO and BANDICOOT). Most possums are about the size of a cat but pigmy or 'dormouse' possums are only mouse-sized (*above). Some of these little possums store food in their tails and sleep in a tree hole all winter with their tails curled forward over their heads. Pigmy possums are brownish-grey with a whitish belly. They are not often seen but are sometimes caught by cats. There is also a pigmy glider (see GLIDER POSSUM).

The most common possum in Australia is the brushtail (*opposite). Its colour varies from greyish-brown to black. It has a thick bushy tail with a bare tip, a pointed snout and long ears which make it look rather fox-like. Brushtail possums live in the bush but they also live in house ceilings and sheds if they can get in. If you have ever been woken up by a hissing, snarling sound of fighting worse than a cat fight, you know what fighting possums sound like! Or if you have ever heard the plop, plop, plop, of footsteps walking across your ceiling at night you know how spooky a possum sounds when it walks around in a house!

The striped possum is black and white. Black and white often means 'beware' in the animal world. The skunk is black and white and it has a powerful 'stink' to beware of. The striped possum also has a 'stink' but not as bad as the skunk's. It feeds by tearing off pieces of bark with its sharp teeth and picking out any insects in the wood with a special long fingernail on its fourth finger. It only lives in rain forests in the north-east of Australia (see MAP).

HOME: Possums are found in most of Australia. They sleep all day curled up in a nest in a hollow limb or in the fork of a tree or in your ceiling! At night they roam about and feed. Brushtail possums have territories (see WORDS) which they mark with scent from scent glands on their heads or near their tails. Each possum stays in its own territory most of the time. A male strongly defends his territory which may be 3 ha and overlap with two or three females' territories. Most female possums have one joey (colour photo 17) each year but the pigmy possum often has twins (see MAMMAL—Marsupial)

FOOD: Possums eat leaves, fruit, blossoms and sometimes insects.

GENERAL: The Australian possum belongs to a different family from the American 'opossum'. The opossum looks quite like the possum and it is also a marsupial, but it has 6 small teeth at the bottom front and the possum has only 2.

Many possums have been killed for their soft thick fur, particularly in Tasmania, but some possum fur is too soft to be useful to humans and, on the whole, possums are in no danger of vanishing.

Quokka

KINDS: Quokkas are small wallabies (see WALLABY) and are closely related to pademelons (see PADEMELON). A quokka is a bit bigger than a cat and has shaggy brown fur, a short tail and hind feet about 10cm long. Its short rounded ears are almost covered by its long fur.

HOME: Quokkas were once found over much of the south-west corner of Australia but now they are only found in any numbers on off-shore islands. You can see lots of quokkas, some of them quite tame, on Rottnest Island near Perth, W.A. In 1685 Dutch explorers called the island Rottnest because they thought it was a 'nest of rats'. The animals they saw were really quokkas and they still live there in large numbers although the island is now a holiday resort. To make sure the quokkas survive on the island large parts of it may have to be fenced off for quokkas only with no holiday-makers allowed or their living places could be destroyed. Like pademelons, quokkas live in thick scrub or long grass in which they make runways and into which they flee for safety. Usually female quokkas have one joey each year (see MAMMAL—Marsupial).

FOOD: Quokkas mostly eat grass but in dry times they may climb up trees to reach leaves and twigs to eat.

GENERAL: On Rottnest Island during very hot summers there is often very little food or water for the quokkas. Scientists have studied these quokkas and found that they can live when conditions are dry because they are able to re-use some of the waste products of their own bodies (see EURO too).

6   Red-necked pademelon

7   Tammar wallabies

8   Parma wallaby

9   Red kangaroo using its tail as an extra leg

10   Grey kangaroo and older joey

11   Young joey attached to teat
     inside pouch
     Photo: Graham Robertson

12 Feather-tail pygmy glider possum

14 Grey-headed fruit bat

13 Banded lesser long-eared
bat resting on a tree with ears folded

15 Eastern native cat

16 Head of platypus showing leathery snout

17 Brushtail possum with young one or joey

Rat

KINDS: Rats and mice native (see WORDS) to Australia as well as introduced rats and mice belong to the Order Rodentia (see ORDERS OF MAMMALS) and are known as rodents. Rodents have two teeth, top and bottom, at the front (look at the picture). These front teeth grow all the time and to keep them down to a reasonable length the animal has to gnaw hard things or the teeth would grow out into long tusks!

There are a number of groups of native rats. Tree rats live in the north. They feed on the ground but nest in a hollow branch in a tree. The black-footed tree rat may give a nasty bite if it is caught. Stick-nest rats build round stick nests on the ground up to 1m high. They are gentle little rats which live in the inland and on islands. The broad-toothed rat was once common in the south-east but is now only found in a few places. It lives on mountains among low bushes and grass. It is a fluffy rat with a short body and tail. Mosaic-tailed rats* have scaly tails and live in the north-east. Rabbit rats are bigger than other rats and have bushy tails. They live in the north and inland (see MAP) but are quite rare. Also see BUSH RAT, WATER RAT and ZYZOMYS.

HOME: Rats are found in almost all parts of Australia. They live in swamps, grassland, bush, mountains, plains, rocks, trees and water. Most rats make a nest of grass or leaves in a hollow log, tree or burrow. In general female rats have three or four young ones about six times a year (see MAMMAL—Placental).

FOOD: With their sharp gnawing teeth rats will eat almost anything but native rats usually eat plants and insects.

GENERAL: Most native rats are harmless and do not carry diseases.

Rat-kangaroo

KINDS: There are two main groups of rat-kangaroos: 1. Short-nosed rat-kangaroos or bettongs. 2. Long-nosed rat-kangaroos or potoroos. Rat-kangaroos are a sub-group of the kangaroo family (SEE ORDERS OF MAMMALS). Bettongs are about the size of a cat and potoroos are slightly smaller. Bettongs hop about on their long hind feet but potoroos with shorter hind feet often gallop about on all fours. Bettongs have bare, pink muzzles and short round ears. Potoroos have pointed snouts and broad faces. There are about 10 species of rat-kangaroos. Here are a few of them.

SPECIES	COLOUR/SIZE	HABITS
Musky	brown/bare tail/body 30cm-tail 15cm/ smallest	N.E./rainforests/day-feeder/musky smell/ 2 joeys/shy/1.
Brush-tailed*	brown/long black hairs on end of tail	S.W. and parts of S./ carries grass in tail/1.
Boodie or tungoo	grey/short hair on tail-white tip	W. and C./scrub/burrows/ carries grass in tail/1.
Rufous	grey-red/hairy muzzle	E. coast/vanishing/1.
Potoroo	brown-grey/white tip on tail	common Tas./once common in E. also/ dense bush/2.

HOME: In the past rat-kangaroos were common over much of Australia but they became rare in many places when the land was cleared and they had no place to hide from the fox and other enemies. Most rat-kangaroos sleep all day in a nest under a bush or in a burrow. Some carry grass for the nest in their tails. Mostly female rat-kangaroos have a single joey twice a year (see MAMMAL—Marsupial).

FOOD: Rat-kangaroos eat plants, roots, bulbs and fungii. Bettongs also eat meat and chew bones.

GENERAL: A potoroo may live for seven years in the wild.

Ringtail possum

KINDS: Ringtail possums are one group of possums (see POSSUM) and belong to the Order Marsupialia (see ORDERS OF MAMMALS). Ringtails are about 60cm long with tails that curl into a ring. Often the end of the tail is white and covered with fine hairs. A ringtail uses its tail as another hand when it swings from branch to branch or when it carries twigs to its nest. Here are four of the five species.

SPECIES	COLOUR	HABITS
Common*	brown-grey, but varies/ tail tip white	E. coast, S.W. and Tas./ bush near swamps and towns
Green	golden-green/black back stripes/unique colour	N.E./rainforests/has relations in New Guinea
Mongan	dark brown/white belly/ short ears	N.E./rainforests/ mountains/no nest
Rock-haunting	brown/black stripe on back/short tail	N.W./rocks near trees/ eats wild berries

HOME: Ringtail possums live in most wooded parts of Australia and in cities, but unlike brushtails (see POSSUM) they never nest in houses. They build large domed nests or 'dreys' of leaves, ferns and bark either in a shrub or in a hollow limb. They sleep in the drey all day. The female (see WORDS) usually has twins once or twice a year (see MAMMAL—Marsupial).

FOOD: Ringtails eat leaves, blossoms and fruit.

GENERAL: In Tasmania the fur of the ringtail is thicker than it is on the mainland and numbers of possums have been killed for their fur.

Some ringtails make their nests close together and the females share them. In one nest there may be two females, a male and a number of young ones of various ages.

Rock *wallaby*

HOME: Rock wallabies are found in some parts of Australia where there are rocky outcrops and caves. You can see tame brush-tailed rock wallabies around Jenolan Caves, N.S.W., at Cunningham's Gap in Queensland and in the MacDonnell Ranges near Alice Springs although in each place they are called by a different name! In general, rock wallabies have one joey each year (see MAMMAL—Marsupial).

KINDS: Rock wallabies are small wallabies (see WALLABY). They are very agile and leap around on sheer rock faces with astonishing ease never using their front feet. Their hind feet are well padded and have roughened soles so that they do not slip. The central toe can be bent down to grip onto rock edges. The long bushy tail is used as a rudder and balancer and is held off the ground when the wallaby hops. There are about 10 kinds. Here are a few.

SPECIES	COLOUR	HABITS
Brush-tailed*	dark brown/black bushy tail	once common many places now rare in parts/agile
Rothschild's	brown/purple back	middle of W.A.
Short-eared	brown/short ears!	N.W. and N./wild and shy
Little	cat-sized/rusty red-grey/ orange rump	N. sandstone country/ cliffs and hills

Also see XANTHOPUS.

FOOD: Rock wallabies eat grass, leaves, roots and bark. They are able to utilize the fluid in their food so they can go for long periods without drinking.

GENERAL: When the little rock wallaby's teeth wear out, new ones grow at the back and the old ones are pushed out at the front.

47

Seal

KINDS: Seals belong to the Order Carnivora, the same Order as your dog, and to the family of fin-footed mammals which live in water. There are two main groups: 1. Seals with ears and with walking hind fins or flippers. 2. Seals without ears and without walking flippers. Seals are brownish-black but they look black when they are wet and it is difficult to tell one kind of seal from another. Male seals are called bulls or wigs, females are cows or clapmatches and young seals are pups. Here are a few kinds.

SPECIES	SIZE	HABITS
Australian fur (colour photo 18)	cow 1.5m/bull 2.5m/ thick soft fur	S./rocky islands/colonies/ once hunted for fur/1.
Sea lion or hair seal*	cow 2-3m/bull 3-4m with white mane	S./colonies/once hunted for hide and oil/1.
Leopard	cow and bull 3-4m/ pale/black spots	very cold waters/savage/ eats penguins/2.
Elephant (colour photo 19)	cow 3-4m/1 tonne/ bull 5-6m/3.6 tonnes/ trunk-like nose	hunted from Bass Strait/ now breeds on islands far to the south/2.

HOME: Seals are found in cool to cold waters to the south of Australia. Some seals come ashore each year for several months when the pups are born. If you go to Phillip Island near Melbourne, Victoria you can sometimes see a colony of seals. Bull seals guard their group of cows and pups against other bulls and enemies. The pups are brown and woolly and gain weight rapidly.

FOOD: Seals eat birds, squid, crabs, fish and other sea animals.

GENERAL: In the past seals were hunted so ruthlessly that some species almost vanished but they are now fully protected. Adult fur seals have a thick layer of fur under their coarse outer hair which hair seals only have when they are pups.

Sugar glider

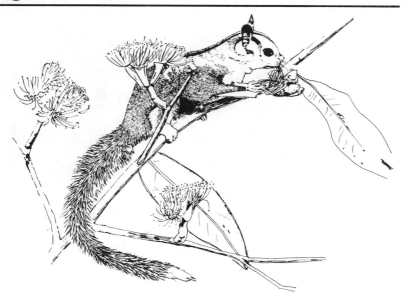

KINDS: The sugar glider* is a species of glider possum (see GLIDER POSSUM). It looks like its close relative the squirrel glider but it is smaller being only about 37cm in overall length. It is fawn-grey to blue-grey with a dark stripe from between its eyes to half way down its back. Its belly is pale to medium grey.

HOME: Sugar gliders are probably the most commonly seen gliders in Australia. They are found in parts of the north, all of the east and south-east and have been introduced into Tasmania. Sugar gliders live in forests in groups made up of a male, some females and the young ones of several years. Each group has its own territory (see WORDS) which is marked by the male with scent from special glands on the sides of his head, on his chest and near his tail. Each member of the group knows its own place and there is little fighting, but the male will fight with any other males which come into the territory. Sugar gliders build nests of leaves and twigs in hollow limbs or tree trunks. They often carry nesting material in their tails (colour photo 21). The female usually has twins which live in her pouch for about two months and then stay in the nest for another two months.

FOOD: Sugar gliders suck sap or plant juices from trees, like squirrel gliders. They strip bark from a branch, puncture it with their teeth then suck out the sap. They also eat blossoms and insects.

GENERAL: A shrill yapping bark made by a sugar glider is its warning or curiosity call; a droning scream means that it is angry and a quiet chattering call helps to keep it in touch with the rest of the group.

49

Tasmanian devil

KINDS: The Tasmanian devil (colour photo 20) belongs to the same family as native cats (see NATIVE CAT) in the Order Marsupialia (see ORDERS OF MAMMALS). It is the only living species in its group. It is the size of a small dog and looks like a fierce little bear with a long tail. It has a large head and powerful jaws. The male (see WORDS) may weigh 12kg. A devil is usually black with a few white patches or stripes*.

HOME: The Tasmanian devil is now only found in Tasmania although fossils have been found which show that once it lived on the mainland too. When Tasmania was first settled by whites many devils were trapped and shot because they ate lambs and hens. They were hunted until they became very rare but recently they have become fairly common again. The devil makes a den under a rock, in a cave or in an old stump where it sleeps all day. Usually, the female devil has a litter (see WORDS) of about four, once a year. She carries them in her backward-opening pouch for about four months and then hanging onto her fur. Young devils are good climbers but old devils usually stay on the ground.

FOOD: The Tasmanian devil eats any kind of raw or dead meat including crayfish, rat-kangaroos, birds, lizards and lambs. It munches up the whole animal leaving only the jaw and teeth behind.

GENERAL: A devil washes itself each day and sometimes basks in the sun. To wash its face it puts its two front paws together, licks them and then rubs them over its face. How does your cat wash its face? Have you ever noticed?

When a devil is angry it makes a snarling cough or hollow bark mixed up with a yelling growl which might make you think the 'devils' were loose! Perhaps that is how it got its name.

18   Australian fur seals

19   Elephant seals

20   Tasmanian devil

21   Sugar glider carrying nesting material in its tail

Tree-kangaroo

HOME: Tree-kangaroos are found only in Australia and New Guinea. In Australia they live in thick rain forest in the far north-east. During the daytime a tree-kangaroo curls up and sleeps in the top of a tree, but at night it climbs nimbly about in the forest. It may leap from tree to tree, climb tail-first down a tree to the ground or jump down from any height up to 18m. On the ground it hops about holding up its tail. Like other marsupials the joey is carried in a pouch (see MAMMAL—Marsupial).

KINDS: A tree-kangaroo's legs are of almost equal length and it moves on four feet much more than do other kangaroos. It has large paws with strong claws, short broad hind feet and roughened soles and a slender long tail (compare with KANGAROO). Tree-kangaroos are one group in the kangaroo family in the Order Marsupialia (see ORDERS OF MAMMALS). There are 2 species in Australia. Lumholtz's tree-kangaroo is grey with a whitish belly, a dark face and a pale forehead. Bennett's or the dusky tree-kangaroo* is shades of brown. It lives in forests on mountains.

FOOD: Tree-kangaroos eat leaves, creepers, ferns and wild fruit. They probably drink water from leaves when it rains.

GENERAL: Aborigines used to hunt tree-kangaroos because they were good 'tucker'. A dog would follow the scent and stop by the tree where the kangaroo was sleeping. An aborigine would then climb up the tree and throw the animal to the ground by its tail.

Tree-kangaroos live in thick forest where white man seldom goes so they will probably survive, but if their living places are destroyed they would vanish like other Australian mammals have.

⌐Tuan

KINDS: Tuans with their bushy tails look rather like squirrels. They live in trees like squirrels too and are so agile they can run head first down a tree. Tuans are also called phascogales and wambengers. They belong to the Order Marsupialia and the family of native cats (see ORDERS OF MAMMALS). There are two species. The common tuan* is blue-grey and about 45cm long overall. Its tail looks like a black bottlebrush. The red-tailed tuan is smaller and rarer. It is reddish-brown and the base of the tail above the black 'bottlebrush' is red. The kowari, another small marsupial looks quite like a tuan and it also has a bushy tail, but unlike the tuan it lives in a burrow.

HOME: Tuans are found in the east and across the south of Australia but not in Tasmania. They live in forests and bushland where they usually make a nest of leaves in a hollow in a tree. The female has from 3 to 6 young ones in each litter (see WORDS). They stay in the pouch for about four months and are adult when they are about seven months old (see MAMMAL—Marsupial).

FOOD: Mostly tuans eat insects, birds, mice and nectar but occasionally they attack and eat hens on farms.

GENERAL: Tuans are now rare in some places where once they were common. This is possibly because they are often killed by introduced cats.

Like most other native mammals, tuans are protected by law which means that they may not be killed or kept as pets.

Up to you

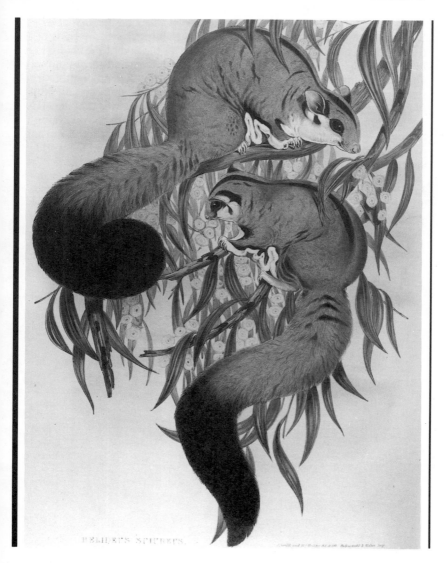

BELBEY'S SILIDERS.

This time it is up to you to do some looking about, some finding out and some thinking! If you go for walks in the bush have you ever wondered why you see so few animals except birds? One reason may be that you make a lot of noise as you walk along! Another reason is that many native mammals are nocturnal (see WORDS) and in some places there are very few mammals anyway. With the help of the map in the front of this book you could make a list of the mammals that live around your home or where you go for walks.

Then divide them into nocturnal and diurnal groups so that you know which animals to look for and when. Would you expect to see a squirrel glider* in the daytime? Or a spiny anteater? (Look them both up.)

All living things, that is all plants and animals, depend on *each other* as well as on sunshine, water and soil for life. All living things are parts of a food chain (see WORDS) and often humans are at the end of the chain. For lunch you might have had a sandwich of bread (plant) and meat (animal) and a drink of chocolate milk (plant and animal). We depend on other living things for all our food and for many other things too, but can you think of any living thing (except for some lice and a worm or two) that depends on us (humans)? Your cat depends on you for food but if you weren't around it would catch a bird or a mouse and go on living. If humans did not exist most other living things would never notice except to find the world a cleaner and less crowded place to live in.

So, if we want to continue to live we had better make sure that we do not kill things unnecessarily or destroy, poison or pollute their living places (see JUST FOR FUN—Abilities), because if we do, we might end up destroying or poisoning ourselves because we might be at the end of the food chain. Ever thought of that?

Vanishing Mammals

Many of the mammals native (see WORDS) to Australia are found nowhere else in the world. Over many thousands of years these mammals have become perfectly suited or adapted to living in a dry, barren land such as Australia. But unfortunately of the 250-odd native species about 50 have now vanished or are vanishing. Animals die out or vanish for a variety of reasons. In Australia some mammals have vanished because their living places have been destroyed by the spread of farming and cities, some have been hunted for their fur or as pests and some have been killed by introduced species such as the fox and the cat. Most native mammals are now protected by law but we must all help to protect them too! We can learn about mammals and observe them to see how they live, we can join wildlife groups and press for animal protection and more National Parks. Here are a few of our vanishing mammals.

ANTECHINUS: The *dibbler,* a hairy-tailed antechinus (see ANTECHINUS) was first found in 1838 near Perth, W.A. After 1884 it was not seen again until 1967 when three were caught by accident, so it is now known that the dibbler still lives! About 6 other species of antechinuses and dunnarts are also rare and some may have vanished.

BANDICOOT: About 5 species of bandicoots (see BANDICOOT) have vanished or become rare in the last 150 years. The *pig-footed bandicoot* has not been seen since about 1926. Its front feet looked like pig's feet. Neither the *spiny bandicoot* nor the *desert bandicoot* have been seen since 1932. The *bilby or rabbit-eared bandicoot* was once quite common but is now rarely seen (see YALLARA too).

POSSUM: The fossilized bones of a pigmy possum (see POSSUM) called *Burramys* (say burra/miss) were found in 1894 near the Wombeyan Caves, N.S.W. *Burramys* once lived in Australia but was thought to have vanished. Then in 1966 a live *Burramys* was found in the mountains of eastern Victoria! A living fossil! Other *Burramys* have been found since and have been bred in captivity. *Leadbeater's possum* (30cm long) was only known from stuffed specimens until it was re-discovered in 1961 in several places around Melbourne. The *scaly-tailed possum* (cat-sized) has a bare rasp-like tail. It lives in the north-west and has only been found about six times.

TASMANIAN TIGER*: This tiger or wolf is related to the Tasmanian devil (look it up!). It was about 2m long with stripes across the lower back. It had a throaty cough-like bark. The female usually had three or four young in her backward-opening pouch (see MAMMAL—Marsupial). The Tasmanian tiger lived only in Tasmania although it had once lived on the mainland. It was ruthlessly hunted by the first white settlers because it ate sheep as well as its usual diet of rats, birds and lizards. Over-hunting and a disease called distemper finally caused the tiger to die out, although some people think it may still be alive in the wild south-west corner of the island.

WALLABY: About 4 species of wallabies have vanished since Australia was settled by white people including 2 species of *nail-tailed wallabies*. The *parma wallaby* (colour photo 8) seemed to vanish in 1932 but then it was discovered on the small island of Kawau off the north-east of New Zealand where it had been introduced. It is now being re-introduced into Australia! The *toolache wallaby* has not been seen since 1924. Also see XANTHOPUS, RAT-KANGAROO, HARE WALLABY, PADEMELON.

Then look up: DUGONG, GHOST BAT, HONEY POSSUM, KOALA, NATIVE CAT, NUMBAT, WHALE, WOMBAT and ZYZOMYS.

Wallaby

KINDS: Wallabies and kangaroos are closely related and belong to the same family (see KANGAROO). You can tell a wallaby from a kangaroo by the length of the hind foot. A small wallaby has a foot less than 15cm long (see HARE-WALLABY, PADEMELON, QUOKKA). Large wallabies have a foot from 16-25cm long. Kangaroos have a foot longer than 25cm (see KANGAROO again). There are many kinds of wallabies. Here are a few of the large ones.

SPECIES	COLOUR	HABITS
Pretty face	pale grey/white stripe on face and under tail	N.E./tame and inquisitive/ holds up tail when hopping
Agile	brown-grey/white face and hip stripe	N./grassland near rivers/very speedy
Swamp	brown-black/rusty belly/dark tail	E./forests in gullies/ bends over when hopping
Brush or red-necked	grey/shoulder and rump reddish	E. and S.E./forests/ introduced to New Zealand
Black-gloved*	grey/white face stripe/ black 'gloves'	S.W. corner/open forests/ active and speedy

Also see ROCK WALLABY and VANISHING MAMMALS—Wallaby.

HOME: Wallabies are only found in Australia and New Guinea. They live in most parts of Australia except the very dry inland. Usually female wallabies have one joey each year (see MAMMAL—Marsupial).

FOOD: Wallabies eat grass, leaves, twigs and shoots.

GENERAL: Red-necked wallabies were introduced into New Zealand in 1870 and since then numbers have increased so much that they have become pests and have to be controlled by shooting. In parts of Australia too, wallabies and kangaroos sometimes eat crops and young trees and have to be controlled, but we must make sure the shooting *is* controlled so that these gentle animals do not vanish.

Water rat

KINDS: Water rats are one group of native rat (see RAT) and belong to the Order Rodentia (see ORDERS OF MAMMALS). A water rat* is about 60cm long overall with soft, thick fur and a white tip on its tail. It has a flattened head, short ears and its feet are partly webbed for swimming. The colour of the fur varies with where the water rat lives. It may be glossy black, grey, brown, reddish or golden. The false water rat is very rare. It lives only in parts of the Northern Territory and Queensland. It is about 23cm long with blue-grey fur and white paws, tail and belly.

HOME: Water rats, like platypuses, live in fresh water. They are found in creeks, rivers and swamps throughout Australia, parts of New Guinea and on off-shore islands. A water rat makes a nest in a hollow log or in a burrow which may be dug in a river bank. The burrow often has two 'rooms'. One is the 'nesting room' and the other is the 'pantry' where bones and shells are left. The burrow usually has an underwater entrance as well as one high up the river bank. The female (see WORDS) often has a litter of 2 to 4, five or six times a year (see MAMMAL—Placental). The young leave the nest when they are about one month old.

FOOD: Water rats feed at night. They eat snails, yabbies, fish, birds, eggs and mussels. To make the mussel shells open so the water rat can eat the animal inside, the rat leaves them lying in the sun.

GENERAL: Sometimes water rats raid hen houses but usually they are harmless to man.

In the past water rats were trapped for their beautiful fur but, like most other native mammals they are now protected by law.

hale

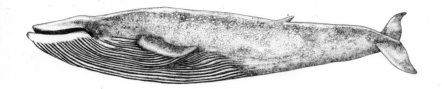

HOME: Whales are found in all oceans of the world where they live in herds of from 10 to 1000 animals. Many make long migrations each year from cold to warm water and back to cold. It is thought that whales guide themselves through the water by using echo location similar to that used by bats (see BAT and JUST FOR FUN). Whales may be seen off Australian coasts and sometimes a whale may become stranded on a beach, perhaps because, for some reason, its echo location did not work properly or because it was sick.

A male whale is called a bull; a female is called a cow and a young one is a calf. In general, the cow gives birth to one calf every one or two years. The calf is born tail first and has to be lifted up to the surface by the mother to take its first breath.

KINDS: Whales belong to the Order Cetacea. About 11 kinds are found in the seas around Australia. Whales see very little and have little sense of taste or smell but they have good hearing. So that a whale does not freeze in the cold ocean depths it has a thick layer of blubber or fat, 8 to 70cm thick around its body. Its tail fin or fluke, unlike a fish's, moves up and down when the whale swims, not from side to side. Whales sometimes sleep lying on the surface of the water and always they have to come up at intervals to breathe or 'blow'. There are two main groups of whales: 1. Toothless whales which strain their food through a curtain of whalebone or baleen which hangs from the top of the mouth. 2. Toothed whales.

1. The blue whale (* above) is the largest toothless whale and the largest animal in the world (see JUST FOR FUN). Humpback and right whales are two other kinds of toothless whales.

2. The sperm whale (*page 62) is the largest toothed whale. Bulls may be 18m long and weigh over 53 tonnes. The cow is about half the size of the bull. The sperm whale has a huge blunt head filled with oil. It is not known exactly what use this is to the whale but it is thought it may enable it to dive deeply (see JUST FOR FUN—Records). The black and white killer whale is another toothed whale. The bull may be 9m long. Killer whales hunt in packs of up to 100. At Twofold Bay in N.S.W. killer whales used to help the whalers by driving other whales into the bay. If you visit the Museum at Eden, near Twofold Bay, you will see the skeleton of Tom a famous killer whale and you can find out all about him. Other toothed whales are pilot whales and dolphins (see DOLPHIN).

FOOD: Toothless whales gulp in water then close their mouths and squirt it out through the strainer curtain of whalebone or baleen leaving any food behind. Most of the food is a small shrimp-like animal called krill. Five million krill were found in the stomach of one dead whale. Toothed whales often swallow their food whole. They eat fish, squid, other whales, seals and dead animals. 12 whole porpoises and 14 seals were found in the stomach of one killer whale.

GENERAL: Whales have been hunted so relentlessly by humans that some species are now vanishing and unless they are adequately protected they could vanish. Parts of whales are used in many products. Whale oil was used in lights for hundreds of years and is still used in soap, skin cream, shoepolish and many other things. From whale bones we make glue, gelatine, bone meal, brushes etc. From other parts of the whale we obtain Vitamin A, strings for tennis rackets, thread and hormones. Ambergris, used in perfume making, is found in the stomachs of some sick whales.

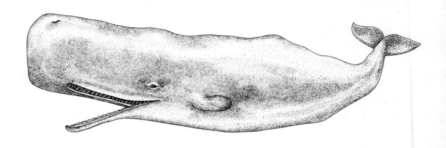

Wombat

KINDS: Wombats belong to a family of their own in the Order Marsupialia (see ORDERS OF MAMMALS). They may be distantly related to koalas. A wombat is usually brown or grey-brown. It is about 1m long and may weigh up to 27kg. It has shovel-shaped claws and sharp teeth which grow all the time like rat's (see RAT) and which have to be kept to a reasonable length by constant gnawing. There are two main species of wombats, the common or forest wombat* and the hairy-nosed or plains wombat. The common wombat has coarse hair, a bare nose and short ears. The hairy-nosed wombat has fine silky hair, a hairy nose and longer ears.

HOME: Wombats are found only in Australia. They were once very common in much of the east and south-east. Common wombats are still quite plentiful but mainly now live in mountainous country. Hairy-nosed wombats have vanished entirely from some places. Wombats dig long branching burrows. They are very powerful diggers and can cut through tree roots with their sharp teeth. They sleep in the burrow all day. It is thought that each wombat has its own burrow but may go out and 'visit' other wombats. The female (see WORDS) usually gives birth to one young one each autumn. It stays in its mother's backward-opening pouch for about 4 months and then in the nest of grass and bark in the burrow until it is 1 year old.

FOOD: Wombats mainly eat grass and bark. Like some other Australian mammals, the hairy-nosed wombat rarely needs to drink water.

GENERAL: Mostly wombats are friendly and inquisitive but they can give a sharp bite if they are annoyed. The only sound they make is a hoarse growling cough.

Hairy-nosed wombats seem to be unable to sweat which may be one reason why they can go without water for a long time.

 Words

Arid	dry, barren country often sandy or stony
Breed	to mate and have offspring
Diurnal	belonging to the daytime; of the day
Family	groups of related species (see below) make up a family which is a much larger group than your family!
Female	able to be a mother
Food chain	small animal is eaten by a larger one which is eaten by a larger one and so on
Kinds	species (see below)
Latinized	a word made to sound like one from the Latin language
Litter	1. leaves, twigs and logs lying on the forest floor 2. a number of young ones born at the same time
Male	able to be a father
Muzzle	the pointed nose and mouth of an animal
Native	belonging to a certain place; original inhabitant
Nocturnal	belonging to the night time; of the night
Pest	animal or plant which is a nuisance or harmful to man
Pollution	something unclean, dirty and possibly harmful
Solitary	alone; by oneself
Species	a set of animals or plants which can breed (see above) among themselves but not with the members of any other set
Suckle	to suck milk from the breast or milk glands
Teat	the nipple or part where the milk comes out of the breast
Territory	a piece of land which an animal or a pair of animals claim as their own and which they defend against other animals of the same species (see above)
Torpid	sleepy and inactive
Wean	no longer suckled (see above); able to eat solid food

Xanthopus

This word is a species name meaning 'yellow-foot'. The full scientific name of the mammal is *Petrogale xanthopus*. The first part of the name tells us that the mammal belongs to a group or genus of rock wallabies (see ROCK WALLABY), so the animal's full common name is yellow-footed rock wallaby*. This wallaby is now rare but it was once common on rocky hills in the eastern inland. It has yellow arms, large furry yellow and white ears, and yellow rings around its tail as well as yellow feet.

Yallara

The bilby or lesser rabbit-eared bandicoot was called the yallara by the aborigines. There are two kinds of bilbies (see BANDICOOT and VANISHING MAMMALS) both of which are quite rare now. The yallara is the smaller kind. It is about 25cm long with grey and white fur and long rabbit-like ears. It is found only in arid inland areas where it digs long burrows in sandhills. Bilbies eat rats, mice and other small animals.

Zyzomys

This is the scientific group or genus name for the rock rats found in the north west and central areas of Australia. The common species (see WORDS) is *Zyzomys argurus* or white-tailed rock rat. Rock rats are one group of native rats (see RAT) and are quite rare. They have long thick tails which are easily broken so they are often stumpy tailed.

All the mammals on this page are different but they have one thing in common, what is it?

Index

Numbers in heavy type refer to main entries
Numbers in italics refer to colour photos

About the Author

When she became a teacher, Helen Hunt wanted to pass on to children her knowledge and interest in the unusual and unique animals of Australia, begun in her own childhood. Her early schooling was in one-teacher schools in the country where weekly walks in the bushland close by fostered her interest.

As well as being a teacher, Helen Hunt has been a fruit picker and packer, a housewife and mother (and now a grandmother), student, tutor and public servant. She has taught professional writing at the Canberra College of Advanced Education, and been an illustrator with the Bureau of Flora and Fauna.

She is now a freelance writer, illustrator and photographer.

Also by Helen Hunt
The Puffin Book of Australian Spiders

Most of us are afraid of spiders, and a little fascinated by them. With this book we can learn which spiders are dangerous and which are not, where and how they live, and how they can be studied safely. Helen Hunt points out that most spiders are very useful creatures, and introduces us to their intriguing attributes and habits. Not just spiders but mites, ticks, and scorpions are also described. All are members of the arachnid family.

The Puffin Book of Australian Reptiles

This book is full of basic information for children on Australian reptiles, the group of animals which possibly holds more fascination for humans than any other. Snakes and crocodiles in particular evoke fear and awe, and are part of the mythology of our country.

In this book you will find out about where they live, how to study them safely, where to find them and how to avoid the dangerous ones!

The Puffin Book of Australian Insects

What's the difference between a beetle and a bug?
How does a tiny cicada make such a loud noise?
Why do flies have huge eyes?

You can find answers to these questions and more
in this book, which details Australian insects from A
to Z. Ants, fleas, earwigs, butterflies and ladybirds
are just a few of the insects described. Each one is
identified with a drawing or colour photograph.
Helen Hunt tells us about different insect families
and species – where they live, what they eat, which
ones sting, which ones are pests and how you can
identify and study them.

Arranged alphabetically and with an index, this
book is a must for all those who want to share with
Helen Hunt in a wider understanding of Australia's
natural world.

Ted Greenwood and Shane Fennessy
Warts and All

Have you ever wondered about those things that
people hardly ever talk about; like picking your nose,
pimples, perspiration or what to do if someone has an
asthma attack or an epileptic fit?

Most people do think about these things at some time
or another, and it's good to know that you're not alone.

In *Warts and All,* Ted Greenwood in his humorous
stories, and Shane Fennessy with his medical advice,
tackle these questions and more, and treat them all in a
fun, reassuring and sensible way.

Also available in Puffin

Special **E**ffects

Exploding spaceships, man-eating monsters, flaming skyscrapers, dare-devil car chases, skeletons that walk, people who fly, wounds that spurt blood ...

You see all these things on film and television, and they look *real*. But are they? Most of them would be either impossible, highly dangerous or very expensive and wasteful to film as you see them. Even rain in a film is not quite the way you think it is.

Here is a fascinating look behind the scenes at the imaginative work of the special effects crews that make it all happen.

Dozens of photos and diagrams explain the tricks and gadgets they use as they invent new ways of showing the impossible.